C0-EFK-559

SMOOCH!
Siblings

Photos by **BONNIE FOURNIER**
Smooch! Project Founder & Photographer

Text by **JULIE MEIER**
Smooch! Project Dreamer (volunteer)

A selection of photographs from

the **SMOOCH!** project.

It's about **Love**. It's about **Healing**. It's about **Making the World a Better Place**.

Dedicated to the love between siblings throughout the world,
including my own:

Janet Evelyn Skoglund

Suzette Irene Abernethy

Ernest Earl Fournier

Richard Eugene Fournier

Mark Allan Fournier

Kenneth Lee Fournier

Raymond Joseph Fournier

and, most especially, my twin sister

BARBARA ANN COLLETTE

whose initial smooch launched
the epic photographic effort now known worldwide as
THE SMOOCH! PROJECT.

SMOOCH! PRESS

The Smooch! Project / Bonnie Fournier
P.O. Box 580404, Minneapolis, Minnesota 55458 USA

All rights reserved. No part of this book may be reproduced or transmitted in any form or by any means, electronic or mechanical, including photocopy, recording, or any information storage retrieval system without permission in writing from the photographer.

Copyright © 2013 Bonnie Fournier / The Smooch! Project
ISBN 978-0-615-90441-2
Printed in the United States of America
First Edition

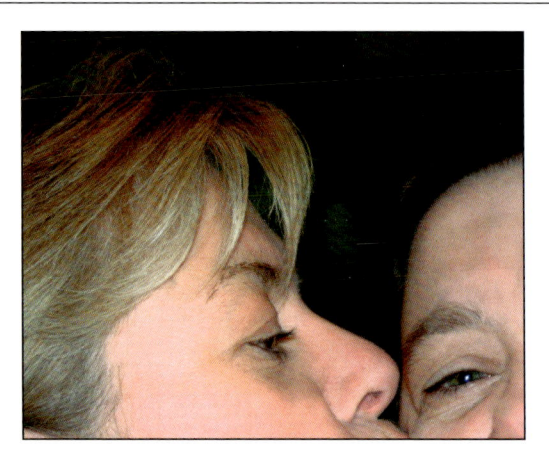

THE PHOTO THAT INSPIRED THE SMOOCH!

This remarkably poor (professionally-speaking) 2004 selfie
of the photographer being smooched by her twin sister
was the seed from which The Smooch! Project grew.

Since 2006, the photographer has photographed
more than 4,500 people and collected
50,000+ photographs, of which 2,000+ now reside
online within The Smooch! Project Archive.

More than a solo creative effort.
Much more.

The Smooch! Project Dream Team is a group of dedicated and
committed volunteers who share the photographer's dream
of collecting 10,000 photographs from around the world.

Dreamers bring their varying skills to the Smooch!
and put them to work on behalf of this effort.
Several Dreamers contributed to the making
of this beautiful book.

The photographer is deeply grateful
to each and every one of them.

SMOOCH! SIBLINGS

I'll be the FIRST

to *Admit* it . . .

1

SMOOCH! SIBLINGS

. . . there were TIMES

when we were growing up

that I *Wished* Mom

had brought home

a *Puppy* instead of YOU.

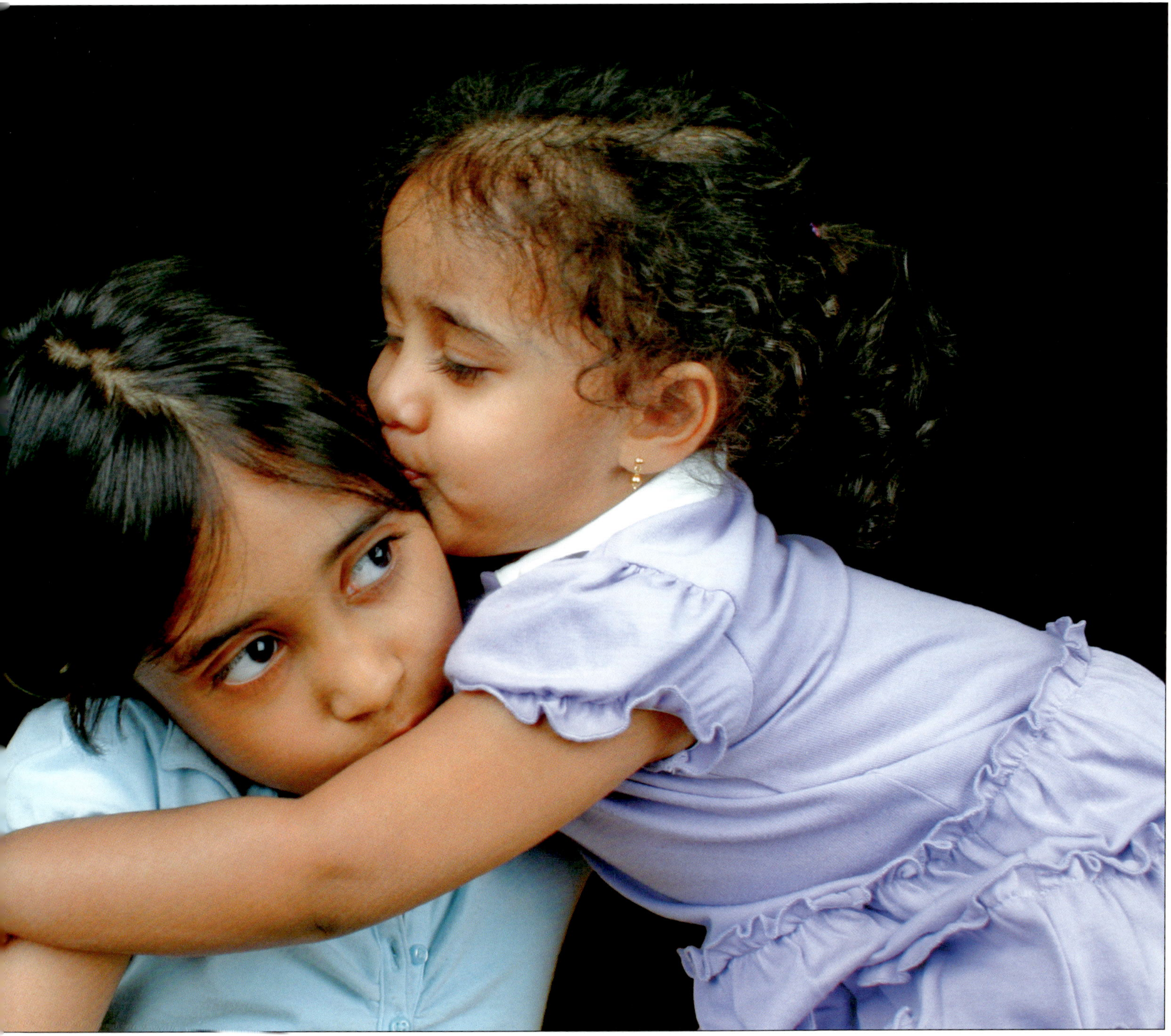

SMOOCH! SIBLINGS

I can recall SEVERAL instances when I really *Didn't* like you very much.

I'm *Sure* you can RELATE.

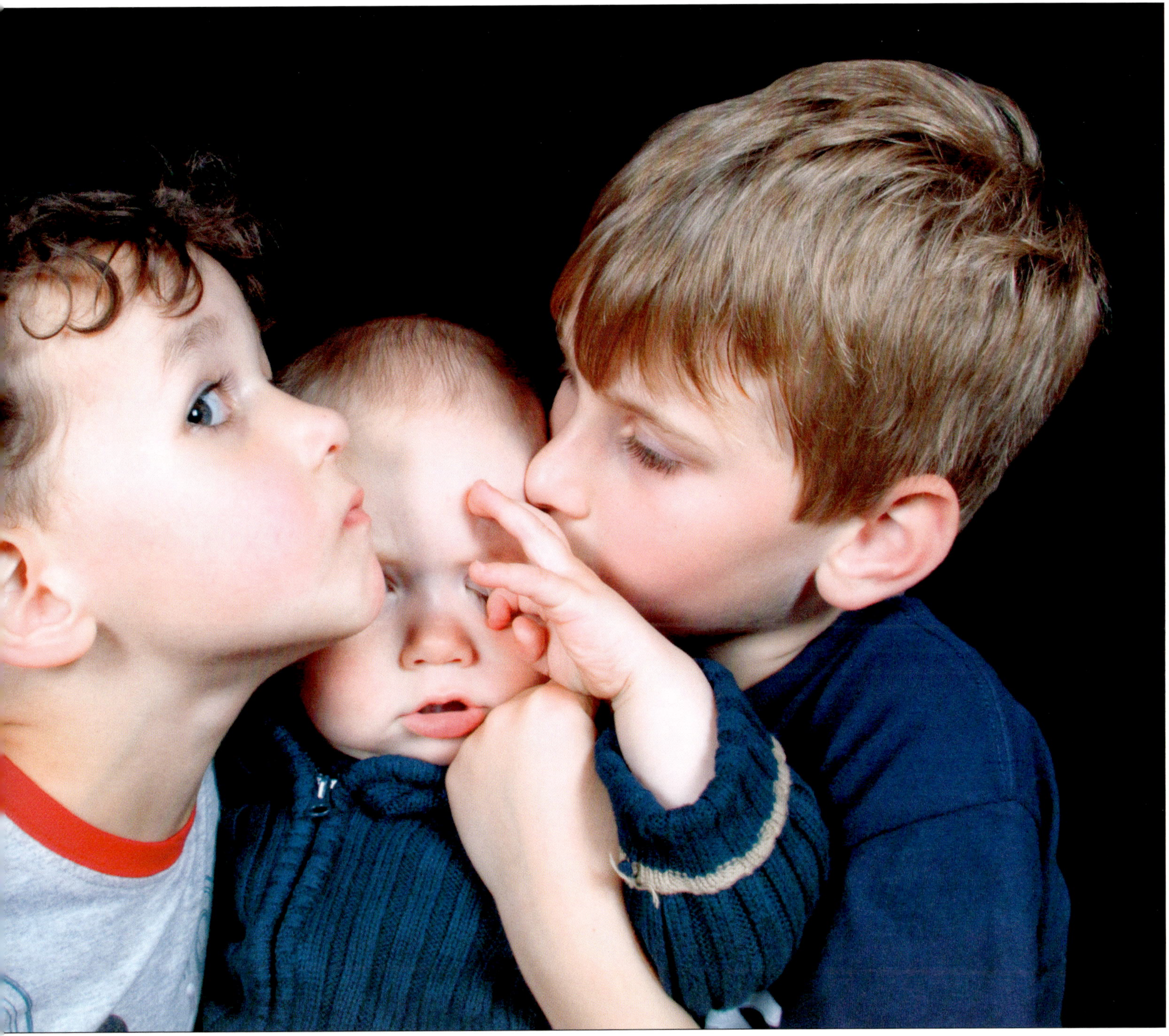

SMOOCH! SIBLINGS

TRUE, you made *Playtime* more FUN.

BUT you *Also* made car trips LONGER.

7

SMOOCH! SIBLINGS

THEN, there was the time *You* . . .

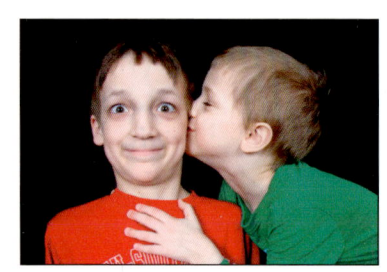

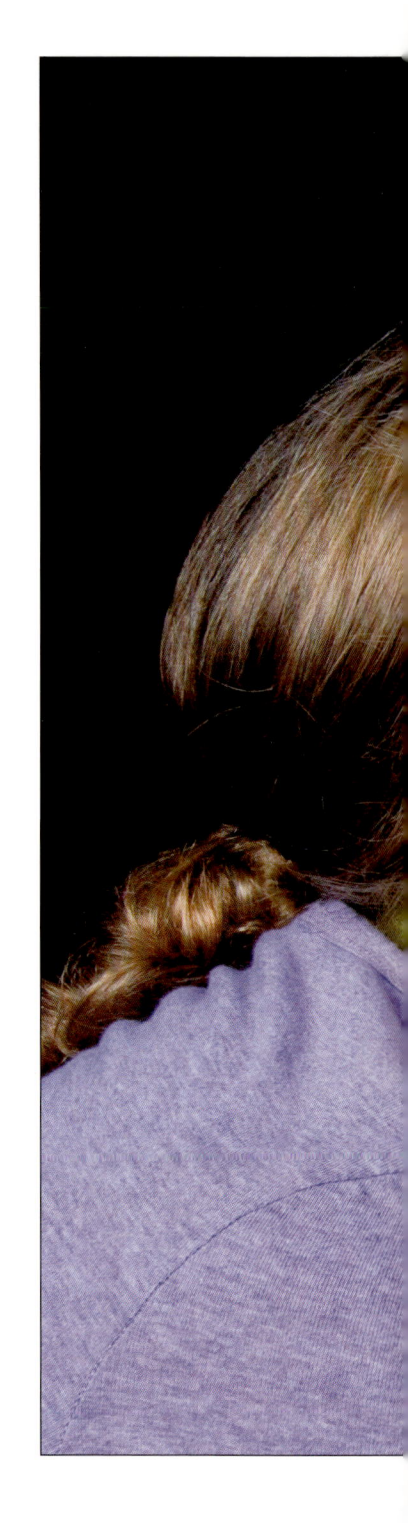

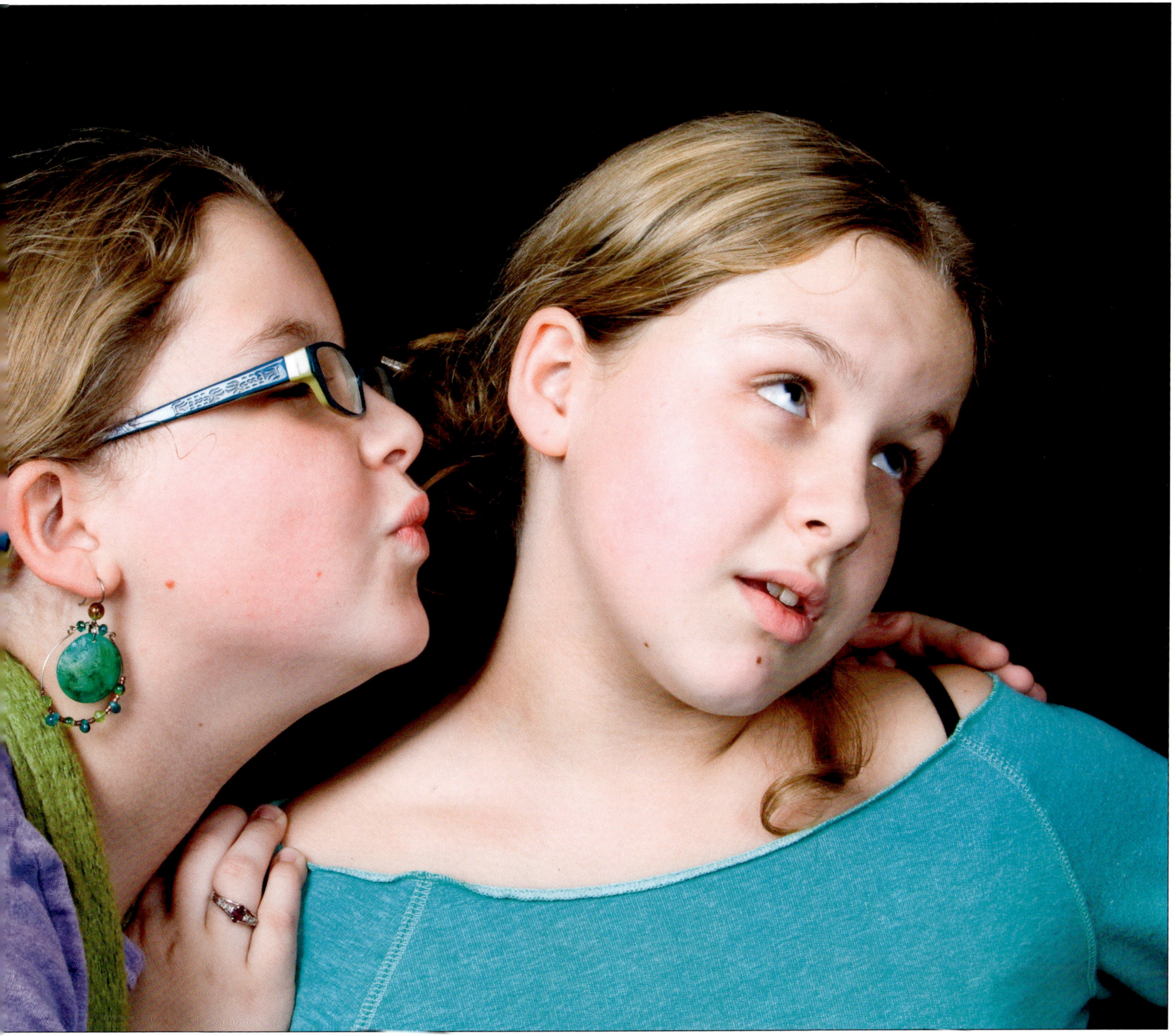

SMOOCH! SIBLINGS

. . . well, no need to go

into DETAILS

about *That* here.

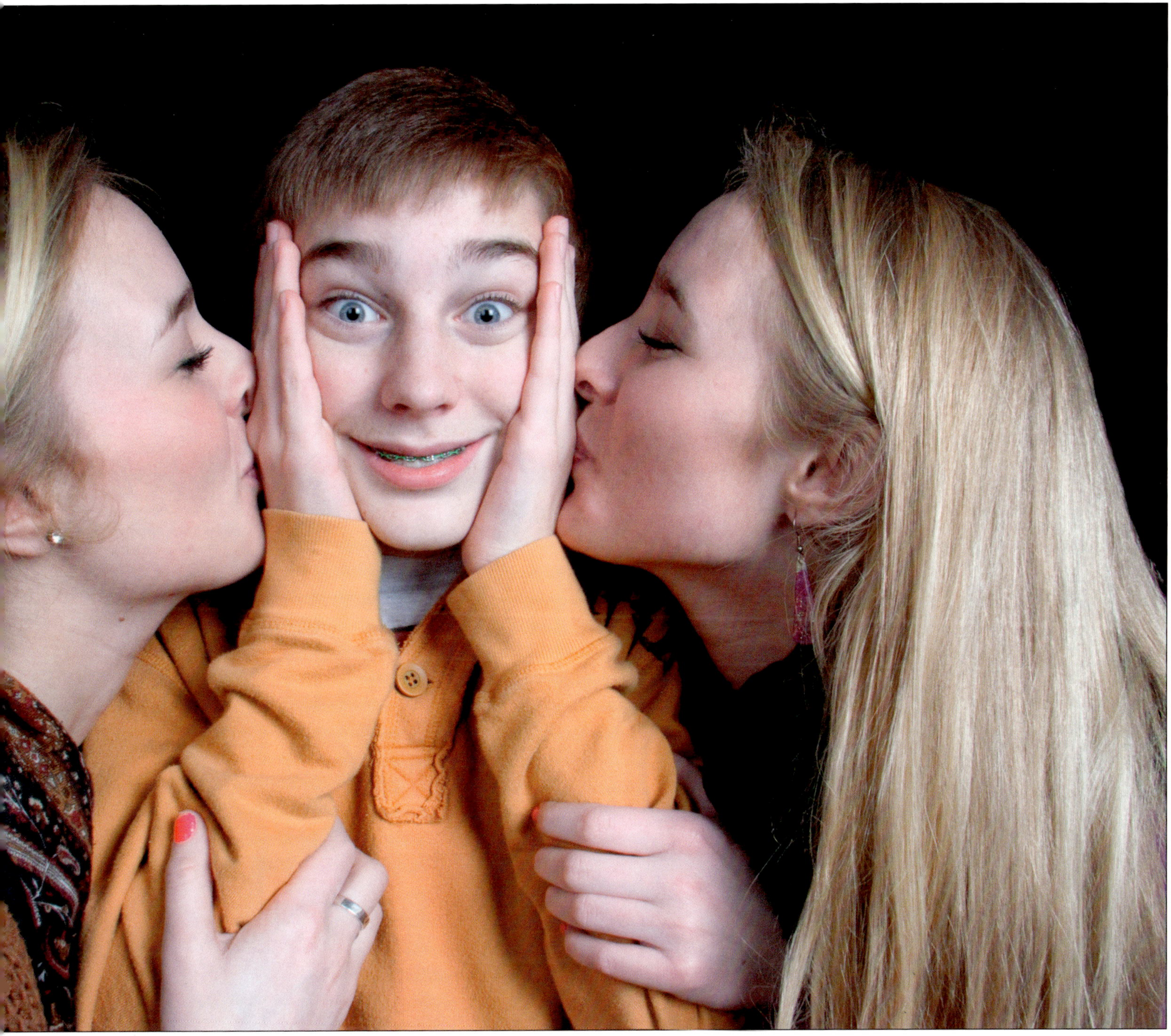

SMOOCH! SIBLINGS

THEN one day,

it *Hit* me.

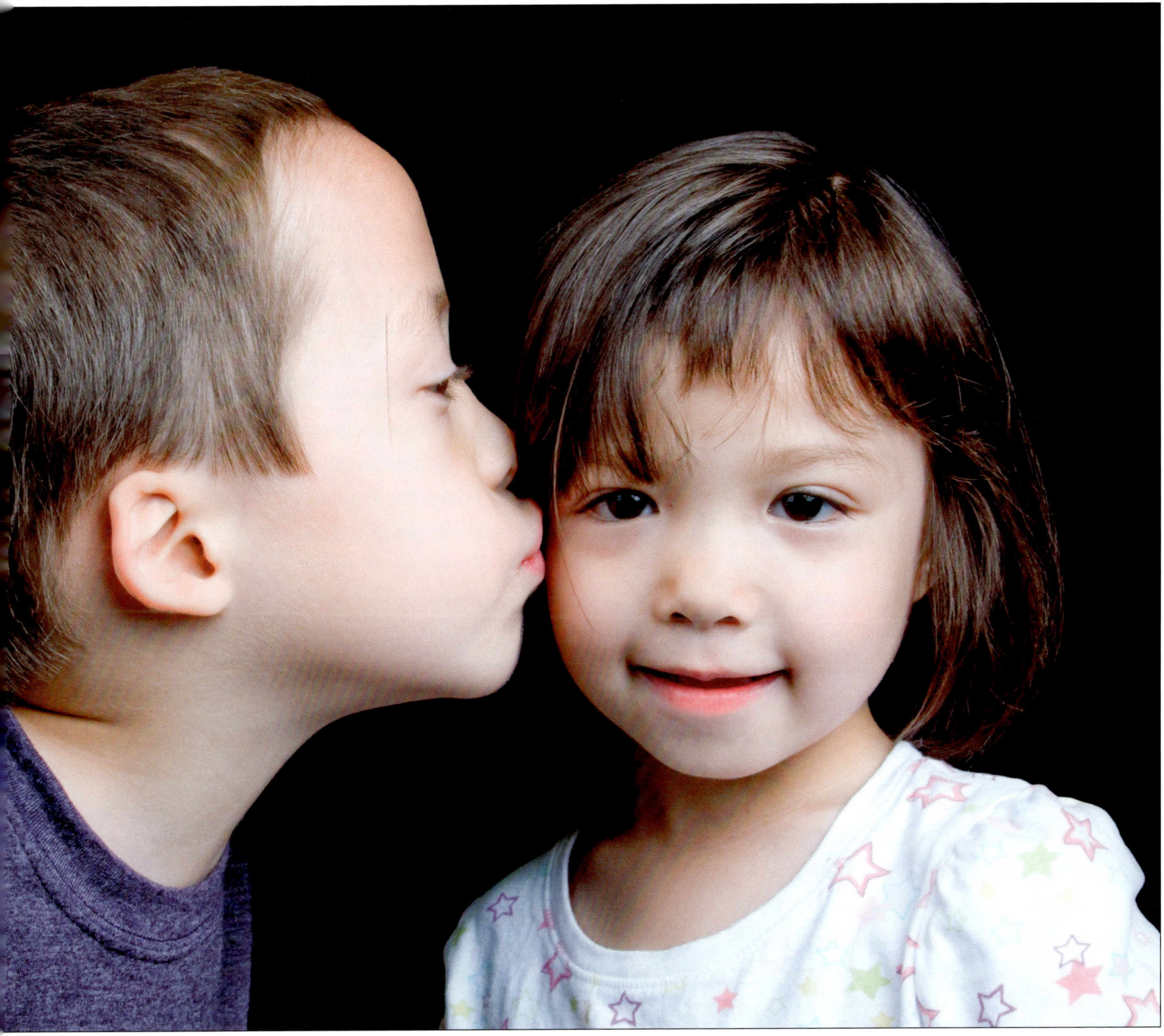

SMOOCH! SIBLINGS

If I hadn't grown UP with *You*, I wouldn't BE *Me*.

15

SMOOCH! SIBLINGS

YOU picked me *Up*
when I fell *Down*.

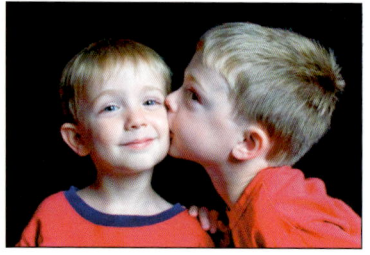

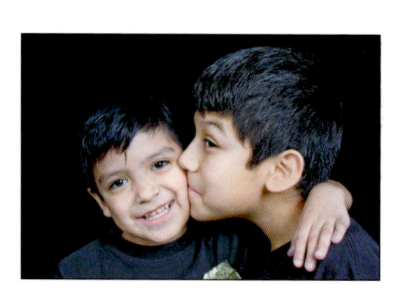

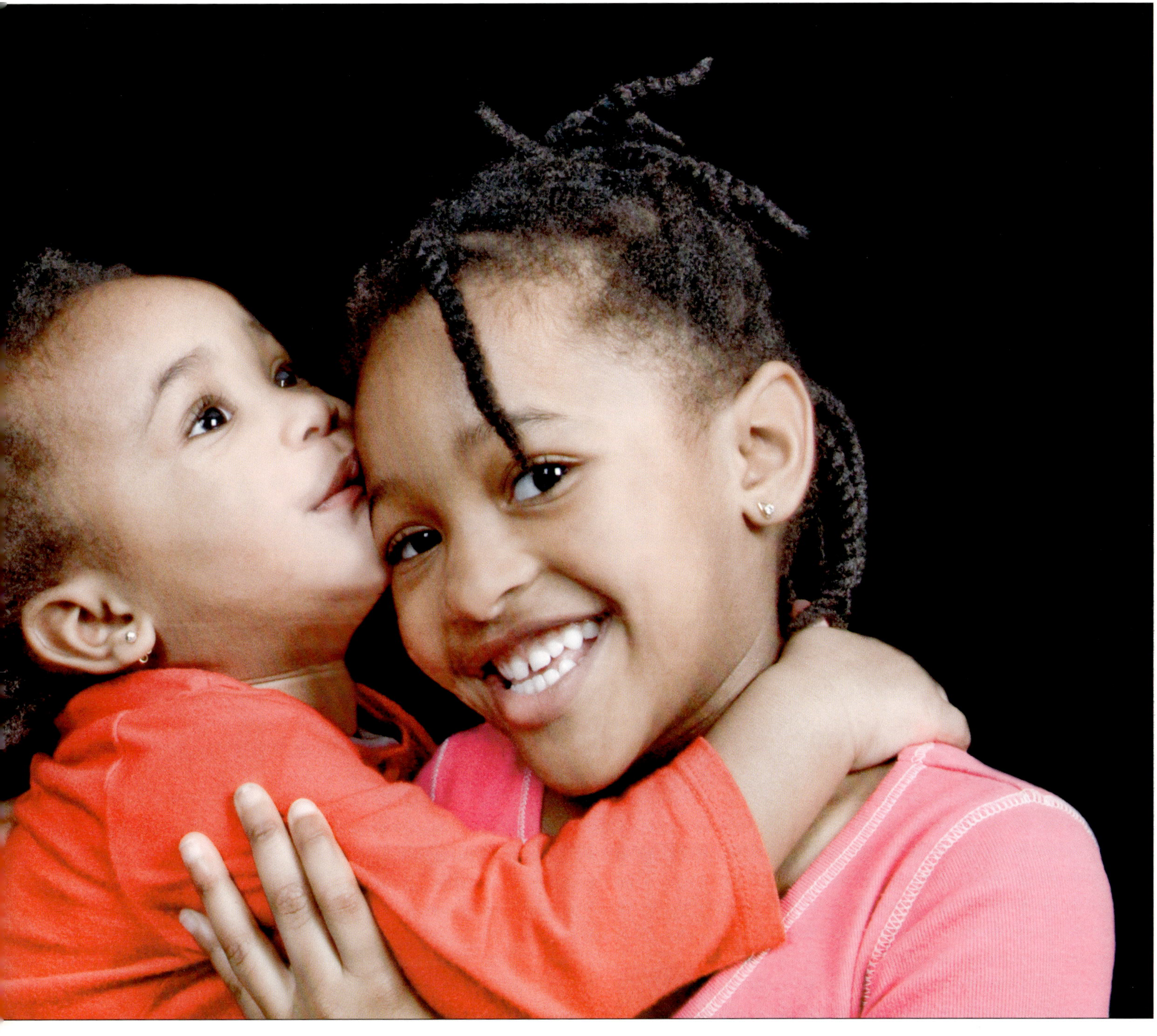

SMOOCH! SIBLINGS

YOU *Stood*

by my side and

HELD my *Hand*.

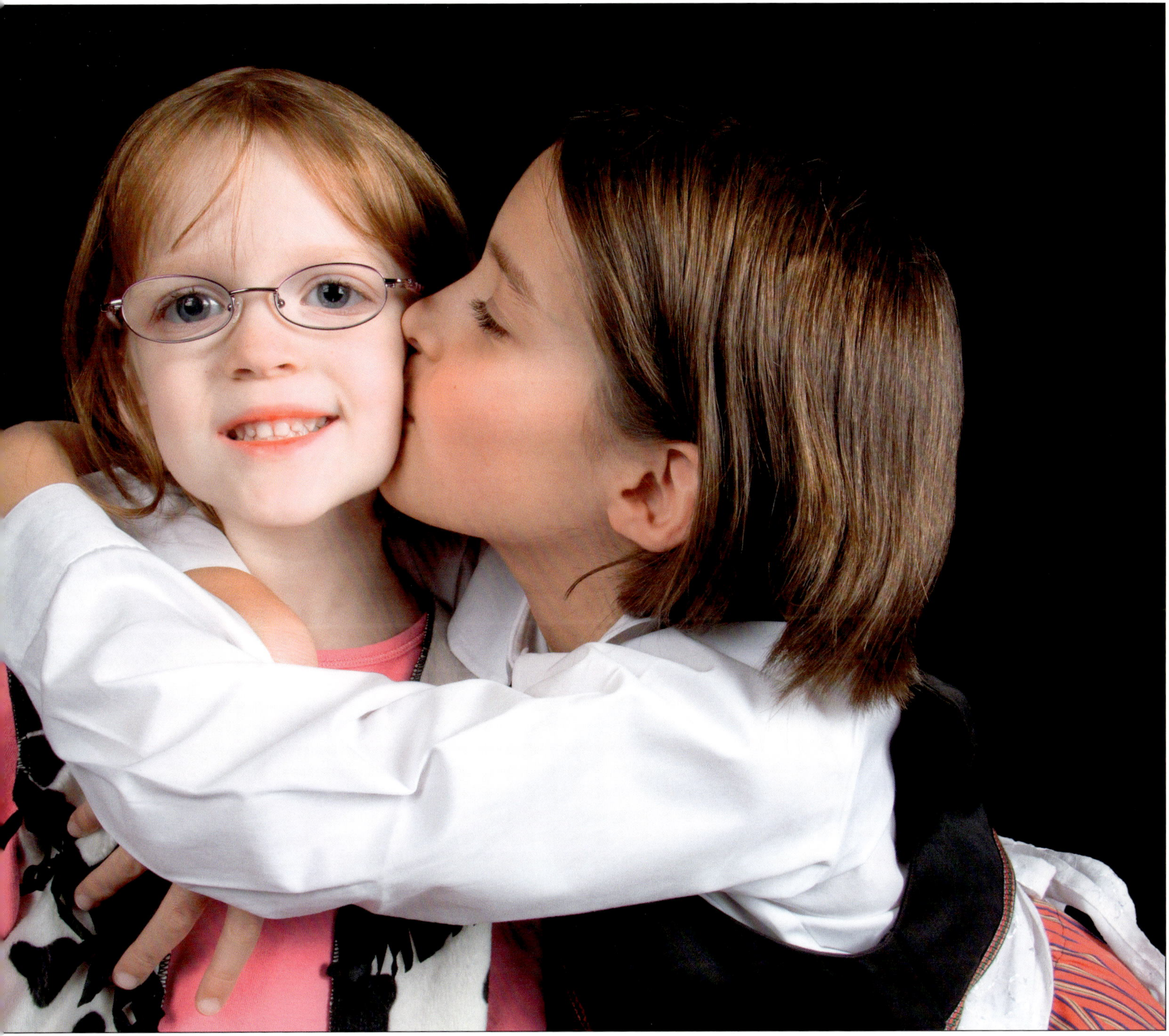

SMOOCH! SIBLINGS

TRUTH be told,

you are a *Gift*

to MY

Heart . . .

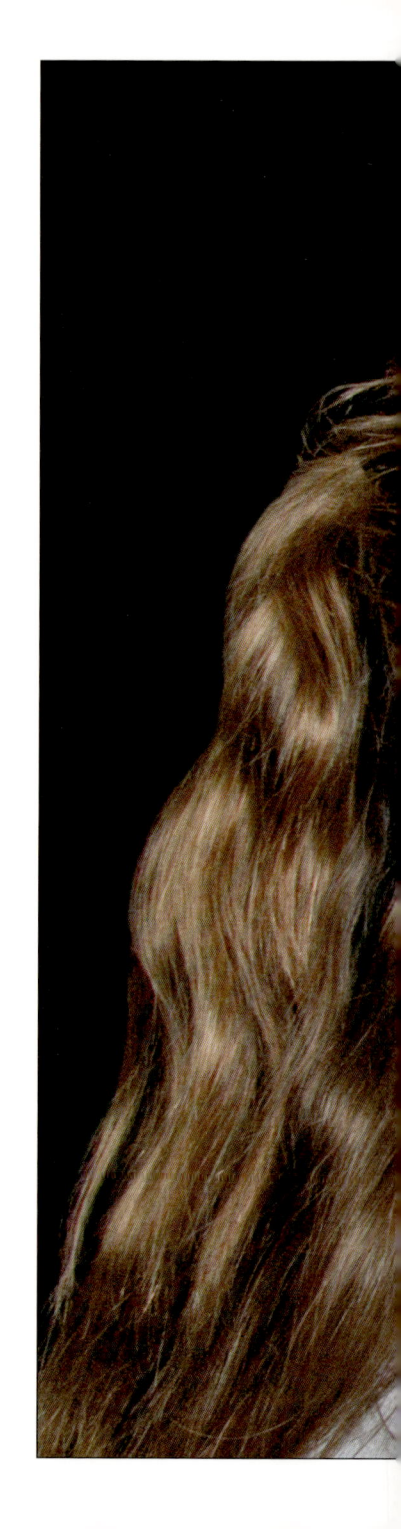

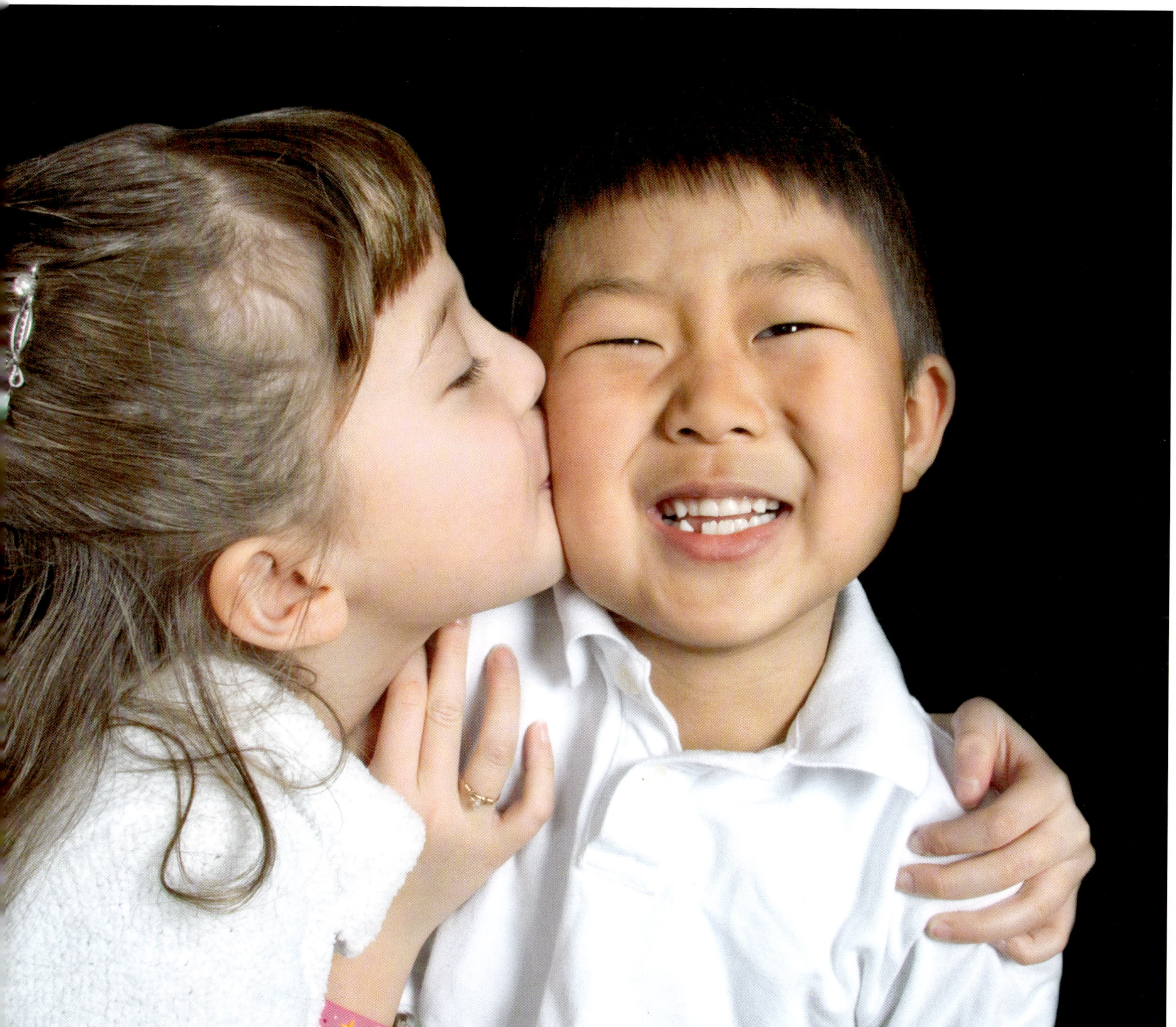

SMOOCH! SIBLINGS

. . . AND a
Friend
to my SPIRIT.

23

SMOOCH! SIBLINGS

YOU make my life *Fuller*,

my smile *Bigger*,

my HEART

Wider.

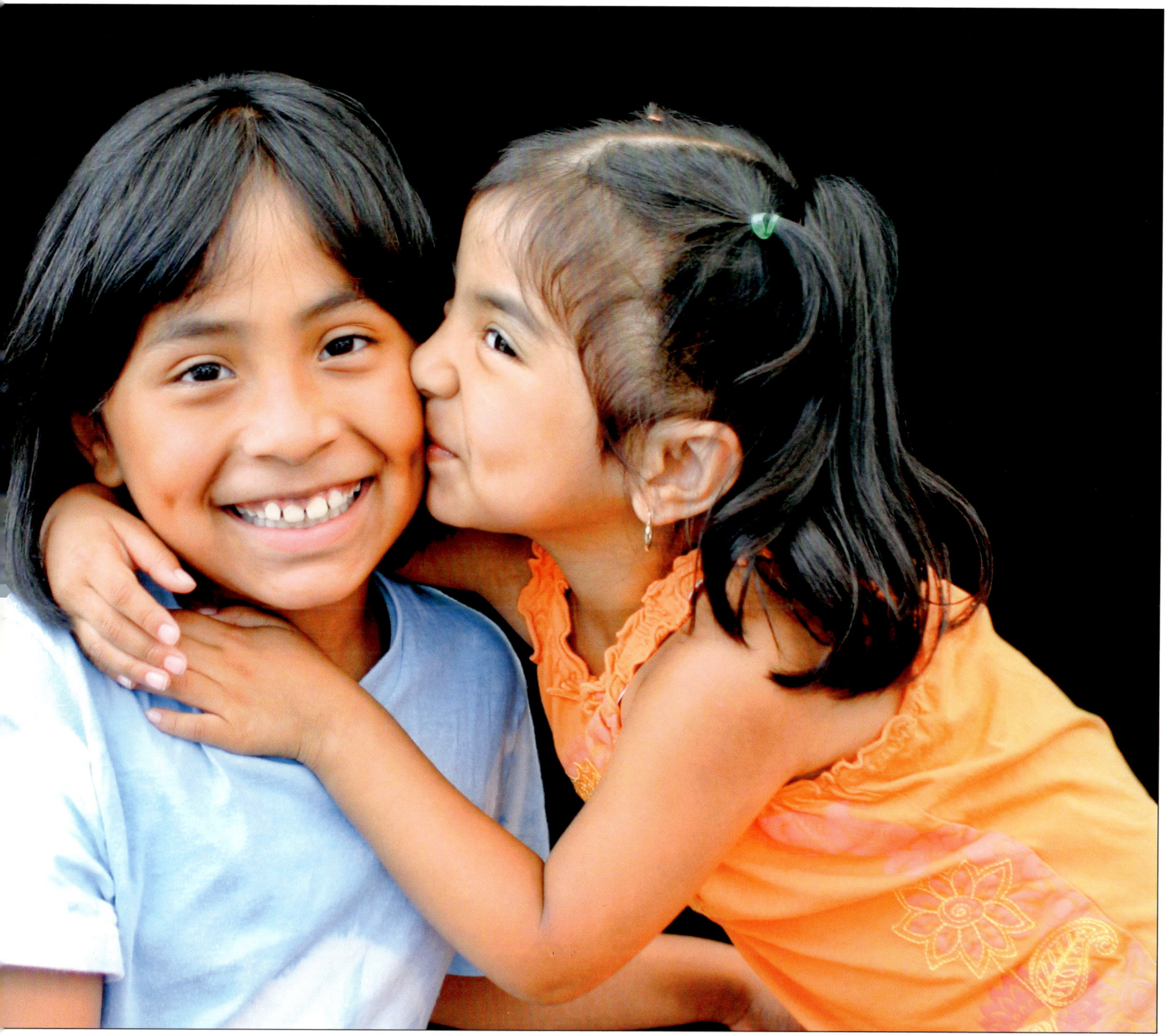

SMOOCH! SIBLINGS

My WORLD is

Better

because of YOU.

27

SMOOCH! SIBLINGS

When I count MY

Blessings,

I count YOU

Twice.

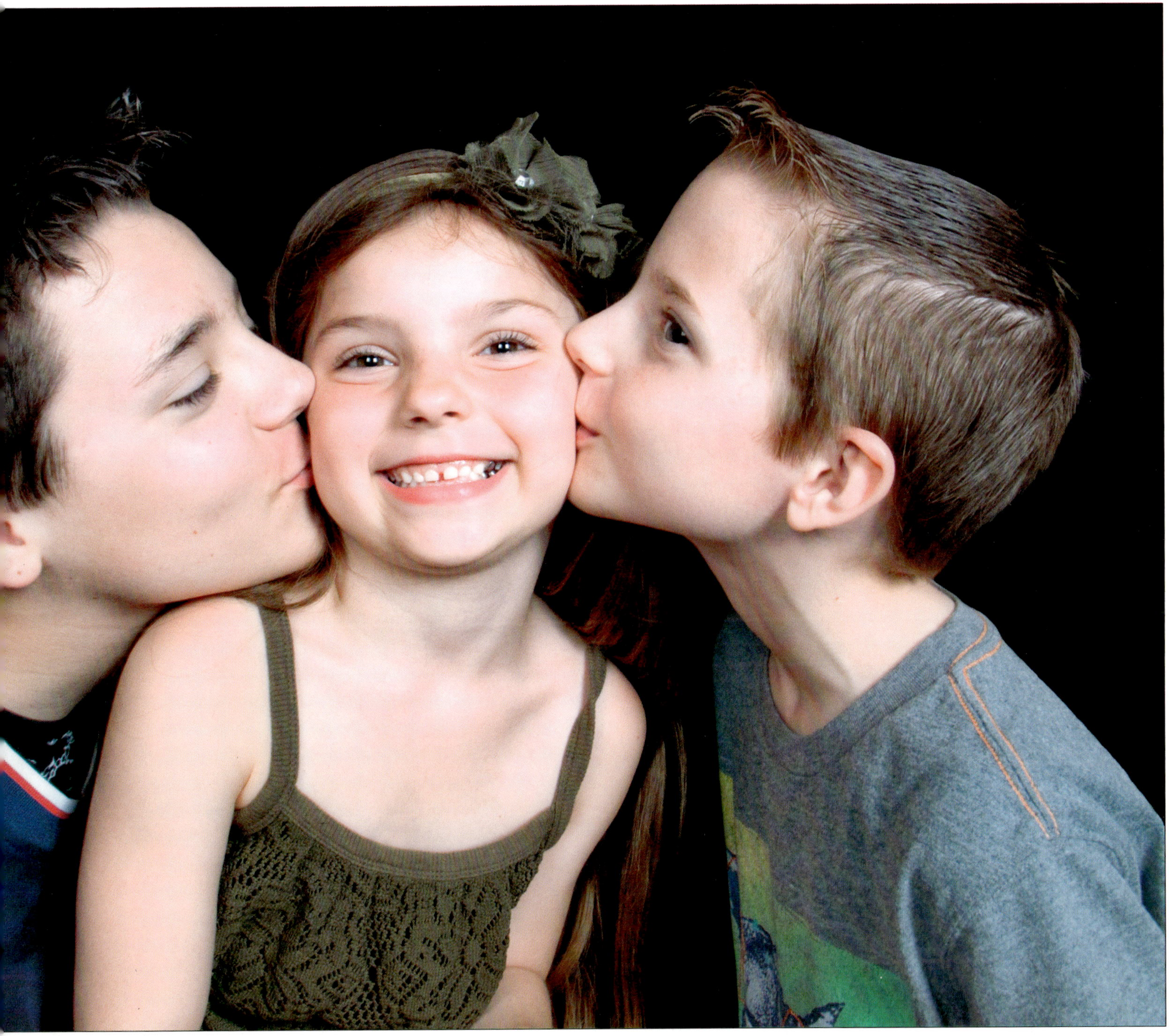

SMOOCH! SIBLINGS

I already KNOW you

Love me.

I wanted YOU to know

I love *You*, too.

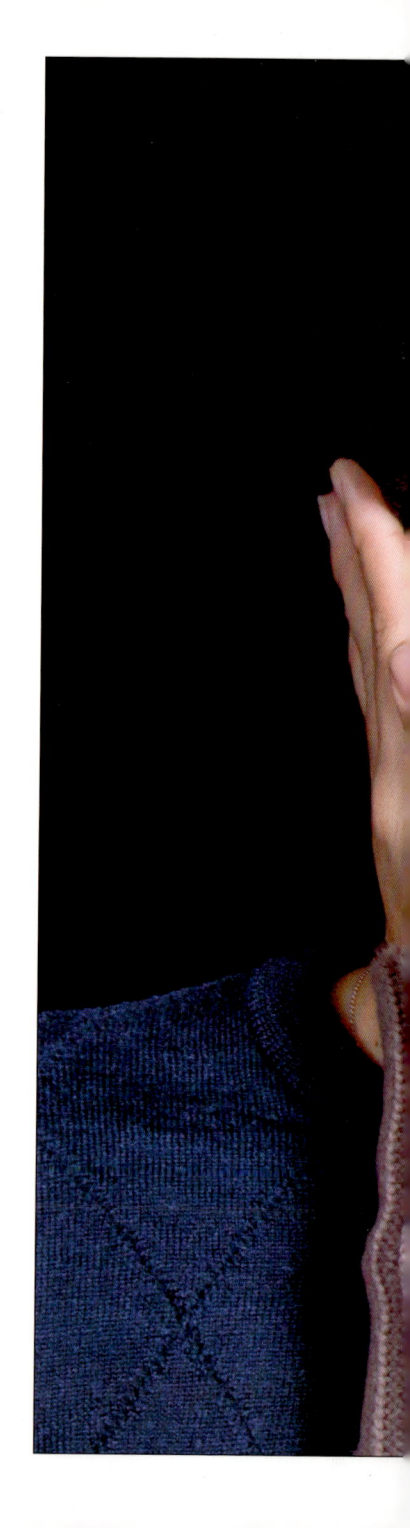

31

SMOOCH! SIBLINGS

We're MORE than *Siblings*.

We're best FRIENDS *Forever*.

THANKS for being YOU.

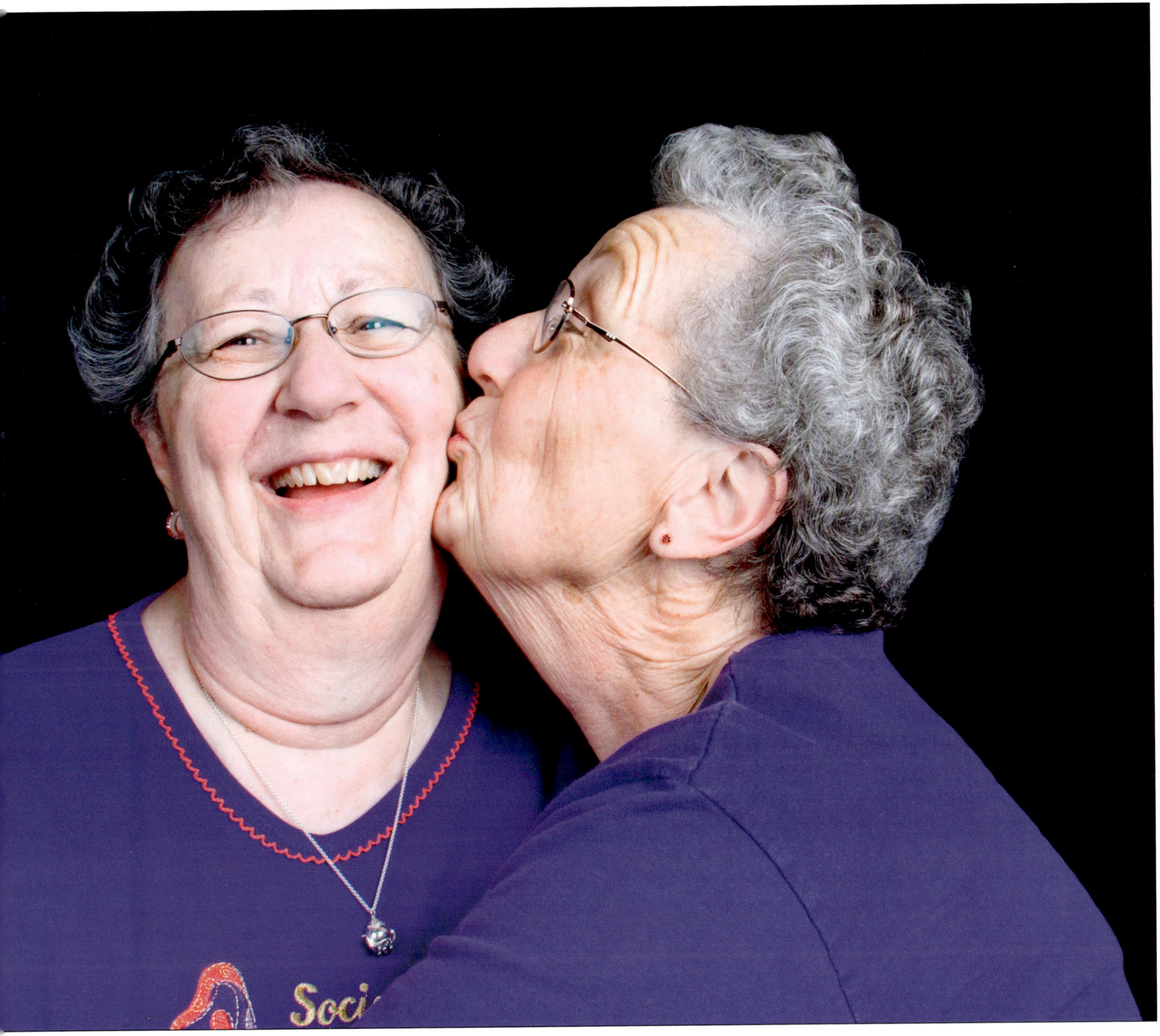

SMOOCH! SIBLINGS: IMAGE KEY

All photos included in this book were captured between the years 2006-2013 and selected from The Smooch! Project category - All in the Family: Siblings.

Classic Smooch! Archive images depict two people.

Smooch! Sandwiches include three or more people.

Thousands more Smooch! photographs can be viewed at thesmoochproject.com.

PAGE 0
Aubree luvs Sean
2012, Demand the Change for Children, Mall of America, Bloomington, Minnesota USA

PAGE 0
Elinor luvs Anna
2012, Gandhi Mahal Restaurant, Minneapolis, Minnesota USA

PAGE 0
Elin luvs Sara
2009, Walker Art Center, Minneapolis, Minnesota USA

PAGE 1
Josie luvs Gretchen
2013, Linden Hills Co-op, Minneapolis, Minnesota USA

PAGE 2
Berni luvs Ofelia
2011, Coronado Public Library, Coronado, California USA

PAGE 2
Mira luvs Ariana
2012, Private Residence, Saint Paul, Minnesota USA

PAGE 2
Ravi luvs Ajay
2012, Gandhi Mahal Restaurant, Minneapolis, Minnesota USA

PAGE 3
Shreya luvs Ameya
2008, Argosy University, Eagan, Minnesota USA

PAGE 4
Natalie luvs (Sad) Brianna
2013, Demand the Change for Children, Mall of America, Bloomington, Minnesota USA

PAGE 4
Dani luvs Charlee
2013, Lake Elmo Inn, Lake Elmo, Minnesota USA

PAGE 4
Makayla luvs (Unhappy) Carrick
2009, Private Wedding, Saint Paul, Minnesota USA

PAGE 5
Elias & Demetrius (try to) luv Gabriel
2011, Duluth Art Depot, Duluth, Minnesota USA

PAGE 6
Malik (almost) luvs Maleah
2013, Demand the Change for Children, Mall of America, Bloomington, Minnesota USA

PAGE 6
Henry luvs Anna
2010, First Annual Smooch! Gratitude Gathering, Saint Paul, Minnesota USA

PAGE 6
Zeca luvs Miguel
2008, Rainbow Families Annual Conference, Minneapolis, Minnesota USA

PAGE 7
Helena luvs Augie (with dog kiss)
2009, Walker Art Center, Minneapolis, Minnesota USA

PAGE 8
Michaela luvs Olivia
2010, Waterloo Center for the Arts, Waterloo, Iowa USA

PAGE 8
Camille luvs Caroline
2013, Demand the Change for Children, Mall of America, Bloomington, Minnesota USA

PAGE 8
Andrew luvs Nick
2011, Linden Hills Co-op, Minneapolis, Minnesota USA

PAGE 9
Molly luvs Lee-Lee (with air kiss)
2008, Seward Arts Festival, Ivy Building, Minneapolis Yoga Studio, Minneapolis, Minnesota USA

SMOOCH! SIBLINGS: **IMAGE KEY**

PAGE 10
Joe luvs Johanna
2013, Shriners Hospital
90th Anniversary Celebration,
Minneapolis, Minnesota USA

PAGE 10
Elsie luvs Max
2011, Midtown Global Market,
Minneapolis, Minnesota USA

PAGE 10
Sanjoy luvs Shakti
2013, Private Family Gathering,
Dhaka, Bangladesh

PAGE 11
Jackie & Robbie luv Charlie
2013, Lake Elmo Inn,
Lake Elmo, Minnesota USA

PAGE 12
Lucy luvs Rose
2008, Holiday Magic Boutique,
The Warren - An Artist Habitat,
Minneapolis, Minnesota USA

PAGE 12
Shibere luvs Meskele
2013, Demand the Change
for Children, Mall of America,
Bloomington, Minnesota USA

PAGE 12
Krisha luvs Dhyan
2012, Diwali (Festival of Lights),
Hindu Temple of Minnesota,
Minneapolis, Minnesota USA

PAGE 13
Davis luvs Karissa
2008, Stone Arts Bridge
Festival of the Arts,
Minneapolis, Minnesota USA

PAGE 14
Pascal luvs Carlos
2009, Walker Art Center,
Minneapolis, Minnesota USA

PAGE 14
Savannah luvs Sophie
2011, Midtown Global Market,
Minneapolis, Minnesota USA

PAGE 14
Maesa luvs Seyla
2009, Walker Art Center,
Minneapolis, Minnesota USA

PAGE 15
Adam luvs Ben
2009, Upper Midwest Living Expo,
Minneapolis, Minnesota USA

PAGE 16
Lydia luvs Daniel
2013, American International
School - Dhaka (AISD),
Dhaka, Bangladesh

PAGE 16
Tobin luvs Abbott
2008, Uptown Art Fair,
Minneapolis, Minnesota USA

PAGE 16
Diego luvs Didier
2009, Walker Art Center,
Minneapolis, Minnesota USA

PAGE 17
Jada luvs Jasmine
2009, Walker Art Center,
Minneapolis, Minnesota USA

PAGE 18
Cole luvs Jake
2009, Upper Midwest Living Expo,
Minneapolis, Minnesota USA

PAGE 18
Malia luvs William
2009, Private Wedding,
Saint Paul, Minnesota USA

PAGE 18
Lucas luvs Daniel
2013, Demand the Change
for Children, Mall of America,
Bloomington, MN USA

PAGE 19
Caroline luvs Cecelia
2009, Midtown Global Market,
Minneapolis, Minnesota USA

PAGE 20
Derek luvs Tyler
2012, Demand the Change
for Children, Mall of America,
Bloomington, Minnesota USA

PAGE 20
Aidan luvs Nina
2013, Linden Hills Co-op,
Minneapolis, Minnesota USA

PAGE 20
Grayson luvs Spencer
2009, Art-A-Whirl,
Wilde Roast Cafe,
Minneapolis, Minnesota USA

PAGE 21
Anna luvs Sam
2013, Solar Arts Building,
Minneapolis, Minnesota USA

35

SMOOCH! SIBLINGS: IMAGE KEY

PAGE 22
Raina luvs Fantaye
2009, Midtown Global Market,
Minneapolis, Minnesota USA

PAGE 22
Kendal luvs Payton
2011, Private Birthday Party,
Saint Paul, Minnesota USA

PAGE 22
Willa luvs Milena
2013, Linden Hills Co-op,
Minneapolis, Minnesota USA

PAGE 23
Savannah luvs Bella
2012, Private Smooch! shoot,
Minneapolis, Minnesota USA

PAGE 24
Millie luvs Birtukan
2011, Duluth Depot,
Duluth Art Institute,
Duluth, Minnesota USA

PAGE 24
Bennett luvs Hadley
2013, Shriners Hospital
90th Anniversary Celebration,
Minneapolis, Minnesota USA

PAGE 24
Tori luvs Ellie
2013, Lake Elmo Inn,
Lake Elmo, Minnesota USA

PAGE 25
Carmen luvs Gabriela
2006, Our Lady of
Guadalupe Church Carnival,
Saint Paul, Minnesota USA

PAGE 26
Kendra luvs Chloe
2008, Uptown Art Fair,
Minneapolis, Minnesota USA

PAGE 26
Jahid luvs Sadhin
2013, MMIC Hospital,
Chuadanga, Bangladesh

PAGE 26
Piper luvs Ian
2011, Linden Hills Co-op,
Minneapolis, Minnesota USA

PAGE 27
Nyla luvs Marlys
2013, Gardens of Salonica,
Minneapolis, Minnesota USA

PAGE 28
Eli luvs Dominique
2010, Waterloo Center
for the Arts,
Waterloo, Iowa USA

PAGE 28
Djuna luvs Hallon
2008, Love Rox, Intermedia Arts,
Minneapolis, Minnesota USA

PAGE 28
Promita luvs Amrita
2013, Private Family Gathering,
Dhaka, Bangladesh

PAGE 29
Hunter & Hayden luv Hailey
2013, Shriners Hospital
90th Anniversary Celebration,
Minneapolis, Minnesota USA

PAGE 30
Jenny luvs Eva
2012, Private Smooch! shoot,
Minneapolis, Minnesota USA

PAGE 30
Julian luvs Ethan
2010, Minnesota Trans
Health Conference,
Saint Paul, Minnesota USA

PAGE 30
Christina luvs Jesse
2011, Saint Paul Art Crawl,
Cosmopolitan Building,
Saint Paul, Minnesota USA

PAGE 31
Catherine luvs Stefanie
2009, Midtown Global Market,
Minneapolis, Minnesota USA

PAGE 32
Rose luvs Judy
2013, Lake Elmo Inn,
Lake Elmo, Minnesota USA

PAGE 32
Wendy & Karen luv Lori
2011, Be the Match Donor Event,
Morningside Community Church,
Edina, Minnesota USA

PAGE 32
Martha luvs Genny
2009, Midtown Global Market,
Minneapolis, Minnesota USA

PAGE 33
Ginny luvs Joan
2009, Twin Cities Live,
KTCA Channel 5,
Saint Paul, Minnesota USA